Faded Roses

By

Waynetta Grant Black

Dedication

To my children

Acknowledgments

To Harrison, who continues to give me my needed space

My writing partners, Susan, Gene R., Ivan and Brice who have continued to encourage me

My 12-year old Grandson, for helping with the cover of this book and Chelsea

And the many friends who believe in my efforts to put words into some sort of meaning.

Thanks,

Waynetta

Table of Contents

Mother Nature

Weeping Willow

Tall, slim, bending and swaying
Bowing down low as though she is praying

Mighty winds blow, but still she holds her own
Weaving and waving as though she owns the throne

Her majestic wand spreads out her beauty glowing
Lithe and light like iridescent bubbles blowing

But why does she weep, this beauty of nature?
Some say-it's to cleanse the earth, so we'll enjoy it's
treasure.

Flower Beds

They solemnly sleep in their darken beds
Looking wilted, bent over, bowed heads

But, others holding their heads up high
Looking forward to the glow of the morning's sky.

Some hum a sweet melody
And softly sway to a silent beat

While the purple Morning Glory stands tall and erect
While saluting the joy of the sun's coming heat

All are yawning awaiting the mystery of the warm
glow of the day
As the dark cloak of night silently slips away
Leaving beautiful flowers to welcome day.

Water Falls

Such glorious splendor life lends us
A constant splattering and sprinkling, like a gust of
dust

It offers choices of grays, blue and green
Such fleeting colors we've never seen

The happiness of a new born
And the joy of a Christmas morn

The sadness of an ill dear one
The unexpected demise of a loved one who's
Meeting his setting Sun

Oh, the waterfalls of life
Carry us through joys and strife

So remember to enjoy the sprays of the waterfalls
Before your Master calls.

Gone Fishin'

I had planned to rest on Labor Day
Stay in my bed and not go out and play

But friends said that I was caught in a bind
And set out decidedly to change my mind

You're going fishing, they said, forget about your bed
I answered, "Oh, no! That's too boring," I said.

Just put on some old clothes, you haven't worn in a while
And before you know it, you'll be grinning' like a "chile."

So, they baited my pole and showed me what to do
It was hard at first, but somehow I got through.

What! A fish! A fish! I caught a fish!
And it's big enough to put on a dish!

Trying again to conquer the task
"Don't talk to me now!," was all I did ask.

With a great big smile on my hot sweaty face
As big as the early morning's sky
My thoughts of being bored while fishing
Had suddenly gone awry.

Pieces of N'Orleans

My folks come from beautiful N'Orleans, (on my Daddy's side).
They are a colorful people with a whole lot of pride.

They don't talk like the folks down here,
Saying "yawse' and "dat" and "dis," while sipping their liquor or beer.

Don't swing like us either, they party LOUD,
Beckoning others, to come and join their crowd.

Swinging and swaying down the middle of the street,
Clapping and stomping to anybody's beat.

YOU GOT A HORN? Blow it!
If you can dance, show it!

Can't sing, then hum
Take a number ten tub, then drum.

Ladies open up them 'brellas.
Throw some pretty beads to the fellas!

Guys, keep the rhythm flowing
As the parade crowd keeps on growing.

You just have to let us be
For we're a great big family.

But, such is the life of these River Folks
Who take the tragedies of their lives and treat them as a joke.

Continuing to try to live the previous lives they had known
But, realizing the wicked waters caused many to continue to moan.

Still, they continue their traditions,
Refusing to make transitions.

But, that's my folks on my Daddy's side
Continuing our family traditions, with a whole lot of pride!

Bed Time.....

My Side!………………………..……YOUR side

(Coolness)…………………………..…..Distant

A slight *shivering*………………...…….A soft and satisfying grunt

COLD shoulders…………………………...A rustling, pul-ling!

Icy feet……………………………….…..WARM boat-size feet

SNATCH-ING!!…………………………...Pul-l-ing!!

Slow-ly movin' to the opposite side……….Eas-ing forward

Back sliding forward and over……………..opposite warmer, slowly inching forward

Humn, OUR side!

RANDOM THOUGHTS

Smiling Faces

You see them at the grocery store
They smile and ask," How are you?"

Replying, you answer that all is well
Then asks of them "What's new?"

While holding a long conversation
About who, what and all
Continuing to solve the problems of the world
The friendly conversation soon comes to a stall.

Then bidding farewell with a smile and a hug you depart
But looking back over your shoulder you catch a smirk
On the face leaving, looking dark.

What just happened, you ask of yourself
Between you and the one just departed?

Where's the warm smile you just encountered?
Did you imagine the joy you were awarded?

Unfortunately, smiling faces sometimes, do wear a mask
But, why? Should we even have to ask?

Broken

Sharp shards of glass from a fallen bottle of milk
Easily slips from a small child's fragile hand
Colored beads from an ancient necklace, threads now bare
"Snap" they scatter and upon the floor they land.

Conversation between boy and girl friend
Plans for a festive week-end
She happily waits, then slowly, sadly awaits his call
While listening for the sound of his Chevy loudly
Coming , but not coming around the bend.

Dana at sixteen years old, runs away from a broken home
Where friends of her alcoholic mother visit her bedroom
She now resides on the side streets of the city
Trying to survive, hoping to escape a vicious cycle she fears is
Her doom.

Our lives are full of diamonds that aren't allowed to shine, Flowers
that don't get a chance to bloom in their time
Promises that are not fulfilled and souls that are broken
But there is a glue that can save these pieces and will mend.

It's a small four-letter word called "love.'

Somebody's Child

Slowly pushing a grocery store basket
On the side of a busy city street
Cars rushing by trying to avoid this fragile woman
Was certainly a difficult feat

Her unsteady wire basket
Was filled with all of her earthly wears
Surely, she belongs to someone
Is there anyone who cares?

A frazzled coat hung from the basket's front like a shield
Protecting her from the many sad and sorrowful stares
As she pushed with unsteady feet, gray head down, shoulders bent
Buffering herself from the weather and trying to protect her wears.

Who is she? I ask of myself, as I watch her slowly disappear
From my rear view mirror
Who was she? I feverously wonder
Surely, she is somebody's child who is wandering aimlessly
Not knowing where or which way to go…

As I step on the gas pedal with blurry eyes
I tightly grasp the steering wheel and scream, "Why?"

Faded Roses

This past Mother's Day, I received beautiful roses
An array of red, pink, yellow and white
The long slim stems were cut slanted at the bottom
To assure they would turn out alright.

Each day I slowly added just a bit of water
For each lovely rose to suckle
However, on day four as I bent down to sniff them
I noticed the slender necks had begun to buckle.

Cutting off at least two inches, I thought
That could possibly save them
As they hung so limply and sadly
On the lovely vase's rim.

Their brilliant colors were receding
And I started to cry for the joy I now lost
They looked as though they were bleeding
I would have kept them alive at any cost.

But faded roses, like a faded romance
Won't survive a second chance.

Simple Campfire

While gathering at a campfire
Looking forward to seeing an old friend
All dressed-up in his best Western attire
Expecting a fun-filled week-end.

But out from the hot embers arose
Faint memories, flickering here and there
Ones he had forced his mind to shut out
But still they lingered in the dark night's air.

I don't want to go there
Too heavy on my mind!
Too hard to bare
Got to push it far behind!

He recalled it was dark there
But, a different kind of darkness
A closet, not for clothes, but for HIM,
A key turned, "Click!"
Enclosing him within.

He had stopped crying out
Quietly accepting his hellish lot
Then a slither of light, a glimmer of hope, and a smile
Chasing away his demonic fright.

Then he whispered to himself with a frown upon his face
As the evening fire flickered like sparkling jewels in that
Summer's place- he asked,

"Why do innocents have to suffer
At the hands of those who are tougher?"
Then shaking his head fiercely and holding it higher,
He relaxed and said, "It's only a simple campfire."

Gran-Maw's Apron

Why do Gran-Maws insist upon wearing aprons around the house?
Is it because they don't want to get dirty while chasing a mouse?

Maybe it's used to dry up baby's tears
While she tells him sweet stories that will stay with him for years

Or does her apron help to wipe the sore of a toddler's knee
While kissing him and telling him stories and what a big boy he's
Growing up to be

Perhaps it existed to wipe a teen's smeared lipstick
As she dashes out the door
Excited to greet her first date with a very special beau

Then, a sadness grabs Gran-Maw, she's a little girl no more
Not long before it'll be time to bake that wedding cake
And out will come from Gran-Maw's drawer
A special apron for that date.

I think I know now, I understand why she wears that apron, see
It's a symbol in the lives of both you and me
It's the holder of the joy of a new born baby's snuggles
And the tear-washer of all life's trials, tribulations, fears, joys and
Struggles.

It is love, worn through all the ages
For Gran-Maw's apron is a part of everyone's history pages.

Signs of the Time

Shanties hanging along a dusty country road
A sorry memory of days gone by
Rusty fences, bent and broken
Sad reminders of how time does fly.

Bumpy pot holes, drooping street signs
Faded Mom and Pop store front
And dusty broken windows
Who once lived there, no one knows.

Just signs of the time long ago
We sigh and re-call how things were before.

Through My Eyes

Through My Eyes
You are perfect
A gentle likeness
Of the Father
Kind, gentle and joyful

Although you have wandered
Astray
In my heart
Perfect
Is where you'll stay.

DAY
DREAMS

Country Ride

While slowly driving along a dusty country road
Playing loud music to rid me of my tired load
I began to take notice of nature's glorious green trees
As I breathed in the warmth of the summer's breeze.

Suddenly I got the weird feeling, you see
That the trees were actually watching me
Some were tall and slim standing way up high
So that they could watch me as I slowly drove by,

Others were closely clumped together
Perhaps for protection from noise or bad weather
And they seem to draw even closer to the highway
When gusty storms find their way from the bay,

They all seem to get along just fine, perhaps better than you and I,
No fighting and fussing and killing, just gazing toward the heavenly
sky.

The Gossip

Where does she work? I surely would like to know
She's got plenty of money, that's for sho'

At night, her house is lit up-full of folks
With sister Susie serving all kinds of stuff, with cokes

She's got a pretty front porch full of colorful flowers
And she and her girlfriends just sit and talk for hours!

At mid- night her house is full of all kinds of folks
Dancin' and singin' an' telling loud jokes.

Wonder why they all use the back door at nighttime?
I don't know, guess yo' guess is as good as mine

On Thursday, all is nice and quiet
But on Friday, it sounds like there's a riot?

And Saturday? Music all day and night
Sometimes, there's even been a fight!

But on Sunday? All is nice and quiet
Guess them folks do finally get tired

But I knows she goes to church and sits on the front pew
With her wide brim hat and whispering "Hi -de-do-o-o."

Folks sho' likes to talk 'bout her house and how she dress
Why don't dem nosey folks, jus' stick to their own business?

Dog Gone It!

Tired, worked hard all day
Too worn out, to want to play
But slowly my spirits begin to rise
As I see those warn and loving brown eyes.

A tail, waiting patiently for my weary arrival
Doesn't know my tired body is seeking survival
A swift wagging to and fro
While yelping and bending way down low

Which causes me to hug and to rub
Always followed by a wet lick from his mug.
So tired, it's been a very long day
Dog gone it, I give up, he's ready to play.

I'm home boy, come here boy!
Come catch it! Here's your toy!

It's been a rough day, but we're ready to play
It's funny how my tiredness just faded away.

Happy Hour

Friends gather for an hour or so
To sit around and just let the evening flow
Lots of laughter, filled with jokes
Plenty of greetings from other folks.

A sip of this, a little taste of that
Listenin' to some good vibes
That's where it's at!

The volume's getting louder
As the gathering becomes a crowd
But, that's what it's all about
Ain't no doubt!

Yep! It's happy hour, time to relax
Let your hair down and enjoy to the max!

Teacher's Daze

Class, please sit
(I've had a rough night)

Good morning, boys and girls
(This dress is way too tight)

Turn to Chapter Seven
(The baby was up 'til eleven)

Joy, will you read for us?
(And my husband just kept up a fuss!)

Johnny, stop making faces and grinning!
(That ole rusty dryer, finally stopped spinning)

You missed pronounced that word, divide it into syllables
That's it! I knew you were capable!

Good Marie! That was great!
Charlie, stop! Or you'll know your fate!

Timmy, your turn to read
(NOW! What does the principal need?)
She said turn WHAT in by two?
(My gosh, is that child turning blue?)
Great, Timmy! You've got an "A"
Kids, see what happens when you don't play?

Now, tomorrow class, we'll have a test
(Maybe tonight, I'll get some rest)

Water?? Restroom?? Wait, break time!
(What teachers go through is certainly A crime)

But I wonder, without a teacher--
The doctor, lawyer, nurse and preacher
Where would they be, without the TEACHER?

First Day

"There goes my baby," she says proudly
While holding back her tears
Salty tears of mixed emotions
Wondering who she'll be
Tears of "she's growing up now
And soon she'll not need me."

Tears of - look how happy she seems
Holding her big sister's hand, not mine
And tears of, I wish she'd look back for me
Just one more time.

Tears, staining my made-up face
While driving away at a snail's pace
But suddenly, I hear a shrill outcry
"I love you Mommie, bye-bye!'
Satisfied, I step on the gas, and smile.

Angel on Her Shoulder

She walked quietly, not a word did she say
While thinking of the fun had in school today
Her number was called, as she boarded the school bus
Quickly, not making a fuss.

Oh, the friends she had made were so funny
And the classroom was bright, clean and sunny
It was full of the work she and classmates had done
Which made going to school, so much fun!

In art class today, she drew an angel
With a crown upon her head
But as happy as she was right then-
Little did she know, it would soon come to an end.

Up she stepped, book bag dragging
Took her seat, 5-year old eyelids sagging
Fell deep into dreamland and one must believe
She saw angels bringing gifts for her to receive.

But it was deep in December, the day had grown cold and dark
And there laid a little brown angel all alone in a locked-up school bus
in the dark!

In her little mind, she started to wonder how this could ever be
Me, all alone in this place-maybe angels will watch over me
She tried the door which was locked, tried to kick it down with a
frown
Peered out a dark window and probably said, it sure is a long way
down.

The emergency exit was somewhere
Angels led her to think-"right over there"

And book bag and all, jumping far down
She felt the cold dirt of the ground.

In the darkness she saw only trees
While hoping she would not freeze,
Ran to the front of bus 119 seeking help
Saw only boarded up houses un-kept.

But crossing the dark lonely street was one dim light
An angel beckoning her and easing her fright
Cold, alone and still afraid and hungry
The little child banged on the door with fingers numb and
A woman looked out and said, "Chile, where you come from?"

A small, but strong voice answered
"Will you call my Mommie, please?"
"I know my number and it's written on my book bag, too"
The little child spoke with ease.

"Come on in chile, out of the cold
Gone on in with my children, you're so bold."

Calling the number, the lady said,
"I got your chile-don't be afraid
She's alright, and here's my house number-
That child must have had an angel on her shoulder."

BABY BOOMERS?

Chill Factor

I looked at him-he was calm, cool and collected
Tried to look away, but the strong magnet remained
What I experienced in a fleeting flash was unexpected
Just had to pull away and get myself contained.

But then the firm stare and bright smile still gently followed me
As I froze in my steps, knowing I needed some distance
Between those lovely dark eyes and that pleasant smile, haunting thee
My delirious and haunting mind, just didn't have a chance.

Finally, moving frozen feet in a different direction
I shook myself, shivered back into reality
Trying to believe it was all my vivid imagination
But why is he still frozen inside of me?

Elegant Lady

On an old park bench she sits alone
Shoulders curved, cane in hand, memory slightly gone

But there's a twinkle in her eye
Could she be reliving memories of days gone by?

Curved, knotted fingers grasping her steady cane
Tiny elegant jewelry gracing fingers that are probably in pain

But a chin held slightly so high
Providing a glance of days gone by

So, there she sits, alone-elegant and sad
Probably still dreaming of the life she once had

When she was the belle of the ball
And all the handsome gentlemen came to call

With grace, charm, elegance and beauty
To always be a lady, she felt was her duty

Once she had won the heart of a handsome soldier
"I'll give you the world," was what he had told her

But then he was hurt and killed in the war
In a place that was oh, so very far

She was saddened, never dreaming they'd be apart
For no one could ever replace him in her heart

So, there she sits, alone, elegant and sad
Probably, still dreaming of the life she once had.

Closed

Where are you? I search for you daily. Why are you hiding
somewhere in my clouded mind, bringing tears?
Have you grown tired of this crumpled cave that has been your private
dungeon for many years?

Do you harbor heavy curtains of sadness because there are lost
memories buried within?
I think so very hard, I look for my glasses, can't find my keys-I'm
often left in silent desperation, where have you been?

I try to grasp a volume or leaf of who or what I've lost
Have I been missing only a few moments or longer, maybe years?
I desperately need to re-call at any cost.

And is there buried disappointments or pleasurable moments-GONE??
Thus, leaving this dark tunnel vacant and all alone?

Unlock your rusty chambers, take away my doubtful fears
Let some sunlight into this dark place of tears
For only you can bring back the old joys
And blissful dreams of yester years.

Help me place the missing pieces of this puzzle back together, or Am I
to forever walk around a prisoner, looking free but
Carrying an invisible sign saying, "Closed-Gone Out Of Business."

Retirement

Moved from a busy large town
To a lazy small town for retirement
Friends looked at me with a frown
Wondering where my good senses went.

They said, You love the noise and the "busyness"
And the Friday, "Girls Nite Out."
I said, it's time to hang it up I guess
Need to slow down and stop running about.

No more rushing and sweating and running late
And praying the boss isn't near
No more filling out forms wondering what is my fate
Can't you see, I don't wanna be here?

I wanna be free, do whatever I please
Sit on my porch with pleasurable ease
So, leave me be,
I jus' wanna be free!

Back Seat Driver

While driving along the busy highway
Trying to enjoy the beautiful day,
And taking in the glorious scenery
While listening to my favorite CD.

Suddenly, I become a bit confused
"You've turned the wrong way!" I'm accused-
"Should have turned left, way back there,
How do you expect to get anywhere?

Wait! Slow down!
You're driving too fast!
And that red light--
How long will it last?

Speed up! There's a long line behind you
With traffic clumped up-we'll never get through!

"Shut up!," I say
"I'm doing the driving
If you had your way
We wouldn't be surviving!"

I say: It's better to be late
Than not at all arriving.

Signs of the Time

Shanties hanging along a dusty country road
A sorry memory of days gone by
Rusty fences, bent and broken
Sad reminders of how time does fly.

Bumpy pot holes, drooping street signs
Faded Mom and Pop store front
And dusty broken windows
Who once lived there, no one knows.

Just signs of the time long ago
We sigh and re-call how things were before.

Seniors

You slyly watch them while looking away
Not realizing that they are what you'll be one day

A slender cane to steady un-sure feet
A fold-up walker with a flip-over seat

At arm's length, they often have to read
While wearing thick eye glasses and hearing aids they need

Their tired old backs are slightly bent
As they continue to wonder where their memories went

Pills, special diets, doctor's appointments are such a bore
But they keep mind and body busy, that's for sure

By reading and writing, volunteering still
Aspiring to do the Master's Will

They've been where you're going
But they're still here growing

Line dancing to the Electric Slide's beat
Or volleyball or soft ball in the summer's heat

Taking up music just for fun
Computer skills and phone games they have done

Classes in art, yoga and just sharing and talking
Counting steps and enjoying healthy walking

Life is what you make it, but you have to be a part of it
Seniors know the secret, that's why seniors don't quit.

TID-BITS

The Silent Camper

(A very short story)

SHE came to my summer camp for kids, not with a parent, as the other children did, but with a person from Children's Services. She had been abused by family members and previous care-takers, then moved away for her safety.

The camp was a horse camp with children running, laughing, yelling and working with horses. But, SHE was still, silent and pale, except for cheeks that turned to "apples" when she was spoken to, but not a word would come from her mouth.

SHE was introduced to Beauty, a gentle quarter horse, which withstood anything a child dished out, pulling her tail, brushing the wrong way, attempting to lead with a hay string, anything to oblige.

SHE slowly walked toward Beauty, never mumbling a word and began to rub her with her hands, was given a grooming brush and shown how to use it. She refused, shaking her head, "no," and continued to gently rub Beauty, who enjoyed every moment. This went on for approximately two weeks, but she did begin to eat with the others, but not talking or playing with them.

When SHE was approached by another child, she would blush and those "apples" appeared, but no words.

Looking at her application, I noticed that her birthday was near. I shared the date with the other kids. They were elated! They wanted to give a birthday party for the silent camper and immediately set to making plans. They made a paper horse and filled it with candy, set up a sack race, had a Pin the Tail on the Horsey, and took pictures on top of a roll of hay and of course there was ice cream and cake .

SHE beamed the whole while, cheeks aglow, clapped for the racers, but did not attempt to run. She did pose for her picture, showing cheeks like "little apples." I whispered to her that I had heard her recently talk to Beauty and asked if she wanted to say something to her friends. She shook her head, "yes."

When we were walking back toward the campers, one of the kids ran and grabbed her hand, hollering, SHE wants to say something! SHE looked surprised, I was too, not knowing someone had been listening. SHE blushed, but softly said, "Thank you for my party. I had so much fun." And then, the apples returned to her face.

Epilogue: SHE completed high school, college, married, has a child, is a productive member of society and keeps in touch on Face Book.

Invisible Invader

I awakened this morning to welcome the Spring
But instead was invaded by an invisible thing
That entered silently through a foreign land's back door
Then sneaked to America to spread evil some more.

Many smiles were broken as lives were snuffed out
Before they even knew the silent visitor was about
Invading bodies and homes causing sadness and fear
Changing life-styles knowing the "visitor" might be near.

No more gatherings at beaches to welcome Spring
Or plans for picnics with family or friend
Stay apart, maybe the silent visitor won't reach us
Fear is the new norm, is what we discuss.

Don't be sad if you're home all alone
Be safe, be creative, check on friends on your phone
And believe in a Being higher than us
Knowing this evil will not win over us.

The Call

Jumped into bed last night, but couldn't sleep at all
A little birdie in my head, kept me up with his sad call.

Eleven o'clock and all is well?? I wonder if it's so…
Then why a sad song just keeps sneaking back and fro
Into my wide awaken mind
While I'm frantically trying hard to rest and unwind.

Mid-night, I toss and turn, feeling cold, but the night is warm
Bathroom call, then some juice, anything to make me feel calm.

Two o'clock, watch television, then try to read a book
But, by then I survey myself feeling cold as my body shook.

Three-thirty, I peek outside and all is still
Then why do I still feel this strange and eerie chill
Racing through my slightly worm and warm PJs
That have always been my solitude for many days?

Then around five-ish, the warm sun dares a peek
But something just keeps calling me away from needed sleep.

Phone rings-so early in the morning??
While I'm still for some sleep yearning?

Jarring thoughts of what's wrong, what's the matter?
I don't want this call and my sleepless mind begins to shatter.

Have you heard, did you know, is it true?

Then I knew…
That she had suffered through the night
Seeking that secretly needed peace and rest
While the calming sun slid silently into sight.

My friend and I had spoken words which I have never shared
For she did not want pity nor sorrow
Of this, she wished to be spared.

Rest in peace.

Tiny, Tiny Tidbits

Mother to six-year old child: Wake up dear, morning is here.
Child questions: Where did night go?

Older adult to two-year old child: You are so-o-o cute.
Child: I kno-o-w.

Second grader note to teacher: My Mom has a baby in her TOMMY.

Kindergarten child: My Mommy feeds our new baby from some skin,
hanging from her body.

Mother to child: I'm eating fruit so that the baby will be healthy.
Child: Is the baby coming out of your mouth, Mommy?

5-Year older: My brain doesn't like "bean-beans." (green beans)

Child: I can't find my other shoe! Do shoes just go walking when
we're not looking?

Mother : Baby can't chew that.
Small child: Can she use Gran-dad's teeth?

Smart small child: If a bear will eat anything, why don't we just make
him eat himself and then we won't have anything to worry about?

Three-year older: I know where milk comes from-it comes from a
cow! You just pump his tail up and down and out comes the milk!

Mom: What would you like for lunch?

Child: I'd love to have "slurp-getti." (spaghetti)

Mother: No fast foods for you today.
Child: Ya mean, we gonna have SLOW food?

In Sunday School

Sunday School Teacher: What's a good Samaritan?
Child: A good Samaritan is someone who falls down and you DON'T step ON him, you step OVER him.

2nd Child: If the Samaritan fell down and he dropped all his pennies, I would make sure that he is all the way down and grab the pennies and run, run, run!

Teddy Roosevelt

My daughter, then about age seven, was given an assignment by her teacher. She was to write a story about someone she loves, draw a picture to go along with the subject and be sure to have a title. She decided to write about Teddy Roosevelt.

She wrote: I am writing about my dog, Teddy Roosevelt. I named him after a great man who was the president. When I call him, I call him by his whole name and people always seem to jump and look around and stare when I call him. Why? I don't know why. But anyway, I love him.

She proceeds to draw a picture of something with four sticks for legs, a long oblong head?? A rectangle for the body and a tail.

After going over her assignment, I said, "The teacher said, SOMEONE, darling. She quickly said, "Oh!" and proceeded to erase two of the stick legs, changed the topic to "Pops," looked up at me, smiled and proudly said, "Now!"

By-Chelsea(7)

Little Black Girl

Little Black girl, where are you going?
Do you know where you're heading with your pig tails flowing?
Are you wishing upon a star, to take you very far
From loneliness and hungriness and wondering who you are?

Have you thrown pennies into a pond
Hoping wishes and dreams will somehow build a bond
With someone or something, that will take away life's sting
Of being that little Black girl, who has a lot in this world to bring.

Here she is world, a diamond in the rough, an oyster harvesting a
pearl!
She's your beautiful, brilliant and courageous little Black girl!
So take her, hold her, teach and mold her, which will take her very far
And one day you'll look up and see, she will be a shining star!

You Can Fly

Take a ride on a magic dream machine
Touch a button to take you where you've never been
Now, close your eyes very tight
Grab onto a star that's shiny and bright

It will lead your puzzled mind to ponder
All the things that you question and wonder
But only birds can fly you say
Oh, just stretch your mind and find that you may

Choose a book, find a nook-let your mind fly free
That's all it takes to fly you to that place, you see
It's so very simple, just try
And you will see that you can fly!